forever
in my
heart
A Grief Journal

Tanya Carroll Richardson

Ulysses Press

Published in the US by:
Ulysses Press
P.O. Box 3440
Berkeley, CA 94703
www.ulyssespress.com

ISBN: 978-1-61243-602-9
Library of Congress Control Number: 2016934491

Printed in the United States by Bang Printing

10 9 8 7 6 5 4 3 2 1

Acquisitions editor: Kelly Reed
Managing editor: Claire Chun
Editor: Renee Rutledge
Proofreader: Caety Klingman
Index: Sayre Van Young
Front cover design: Ashley Prine
Cover art: butterflies © Yoko Design/shutterstock.com;
    texture in type © Natalia-flurno/shutterstock.com
Interior design: what!design @ whatweb.com
Interior art: © gorbach elena/shutterstock.com; © Aboard/shutterstock.com

Distributed by Publishers Group West

In memory of Jana Denise Carroll and Jan Stanfield Davis

This journal is dedicated to the loving memory of:

_____

Contents

Introduction

Those dear to us who have passed on are forever in our hearts—we treasure memories of departed loved ones, think about them often, and still love them deeply. This journal is a way for you to pick one of these precious people and dedicate some time to savoring and recording those memories, thoughts, and feelings. There is also space in this journal for you to get in touch with some of the blessings that have come into your life since your loved one died, and think about your goals for the future.

But this journal is also much more. It's a way for you to acknowledge that while loved ones who have passed on are still in our hearts, they are also still in our lives. Death brings the following paradox: loved ones who have passed are gone, yet they are not gone. As you write in the pages of this journal, the loved one you have dedicated the journal to will be watching from their vantage point in heaven, reading every word. This journal will help you feel the presence of your loved one's spirit even more and communicate with them in a unique way; sending your loved one messages, sharing what's on your mind and in your heart, and asking your loved one for signs of their continued existence in your life.

And remember, this journal is a work in progress. If you can't think of a way to respond to a prompt when you first sit down and read the journal, leave that prompt blank for now. Then, when you get a sign from your loved one or a memory comes flooding back that fits this particular prompt, you can grab your journal and fill it out. Every time you fill out a prompt, the bond between you and your departed loved one will grow stronger, and you will feel their presence draw closer.

When I learned from my publisher that this journal would come out in November I had to smile. My mother, Jana, was born in November and passed away 25 years ago on October 31. The date the publisher had chosen to put out this journal seemed like a sign from her. My parents divorced when I was very young, and at the time of her death I was living with my father because my mother and I were estranged. Her terminal illness had taken its toll not only on her body and spirit, but on our relationship—yet our separation was about much more than that. I was only 17 when she passed away, so it wasn't until I became an adult and started talking to friends, loved ones, and a trusted therapist that I realized how angry I was at my mother, not for becoming ill and abandoning me (which was out of her control, obviously), but for an abandonment that started long before that illness.

I tell you all this not to disparage my mother's character, as she was in many ways a wonderful, strong, intelligent, funny, generous, compassionate, independent, brave, and warm woman who was much admired and loved. I tell you the full story of our relationship to try and convey just how miraculous it was that our relationship was rekindled, and healed, only after her passing from this earth. It was only after my mother died that we became close: I began to sense her presence, feel her spirit, and reach out to her for courage, advice, and nurturing in a way that I never felt allowed to do, or felt was quite reciprocated, while she was alive.

Staring at my mother's picture one day when I was 19 and listening to one of her favorite songs, "Bridge Over Troubled Water," I cried for what seemed like a whole afternoon, telling her in between sobs how much I wished I had a mother who was alive and could protect and guide me. Ever since that day, when I am particularly down or confused, I will hear the song "Bridge Over Troubled Water" out of the blue at restaurants, in stores, or on a car radio. I intuitively know it is my mother playing DJ, reminding me that she is in fact guiding and protecting me now from heaven.

My mom has become a trusted confidant, and I talk to her often these days—even hearing and feeling her answers in reply. I know she is sorry for hurting me, and I am sorry that she didn't have an easier life. Today she is the parent I always craved, sending me wisdom, fighting my battles, loving me unconditionally, and being my biggest cheerleader from heaven.

They say that souls who pass over retain much of the same personality they had when they were on earth in human form. While I believe that is true, I also believe that in heaven we are more compassionate, more enlightened, more forgiving. If you have unresolved issues with a loved one, don't be afraid to be honest with them in the pages of this journal. Nothing can be healed until it is revealed. So please reveal everything in this journal—all the love and good memories, but also all the pain, fear, and frustration. All the things you said to your loved one when they were alive, and all the things that were left unsaid. Losing someone close to us creates many complex emotional responses, and this journal is a perfect place to examine those emotions and start to work through them.

Be sure to fill out the dedication to your loved one on the first page. I am personally dedicating this journal to two very special, much-loved mothers, Jana Denise Carroll and Jan Stanfield Davis.

I thank you for picking up this guided journal, and I know your departed loved one thanks you too. Putting your pen to paper on the first page of this journal is the beginning of a closer relationship between you and your departed loved one, the beginning of an exciting, sacred, healing journey for both of you.

All my love and many blessings,
Tanya

CHAPTER 1

You Are Forever in My Heart...
and That's Why I Can Still
Feel You Here with Me

*I can still feel you here with me when I spend
time with the people, places, and things you love.*

I blare your favorite music, then sing or dance around the
room, and know you are jamming along with me on songs like

_____

_____

_____

_____.

Curling up and listening to this favorite song of yours when I
am really missing you brings happy tears to my eyes:

_____

_____.

forever in my heart

This movie always reminds me of you: _____

_____

_____.

Can you guess how many times I've seen it?

There are days when I stare at the cover of one of your favorite books or open to a random page and read a paragraph to feel closer to you. Today I opened to a random page of this favorite book of yours: _____

_____.

This was the first sentence I saw:

_____

_____

_____

_____.

My favorite character/insight from this book is _____

_____

_____.

Sipping a cup of morning mojo at _____

_____

reminds me of you. My favorite drink at this coffee shop is __

_____.

Right now I bet you're craving their _____

_____.

Sometimes I eat at your favorite restaurant, _____

_____,

and order your usual, the _____

_____.

Once in a while I will eat your favorite snack, _____

_____.

It was never one of my favorites, but just going to the store
and buying it, or the ingredients to prepare it, makes you feel
closer.

forever in my heart

Meals that I find myself cooking when I am missing you:

_____

_____

_____

_____.

When I bake _____

_____

the house smells of _____

_____,

which reminds me of when we _____

_____

_____

_____.

Browsing at this record/bookstore reminds me of you:

_____

_____

_____.

When I shop at this clothing store I see so many things that scream your name:

_____

_____

_____.

Last time I was there I picked up this great _____

_____

that you would love.

I keep a bottle of this perfume/cologne that you used to wear:

_____.

When I spray a little in the air it's like you suddenly materialize before me.

forever in my heart

Recently I caught a whiff of this scent by surprise when I was

_____

_____

at _____,

and it made me smile and wonder if it was a sign from you
from heaven.

Could you send me a sign from heaven sometime in the form
of a special scent? When you do, I will come back and record
the moment here: _____

_____

_____

_____

_____

_____.

Strolling along this beach, sitting beside this lake, or dipping my toes in this pond makes me think of you:

_____.

It reminds me of the time we _____

_____

_____

_____.

I love _____

because it was your favorite season. Activities I like to do this

time of year include _____

_____

_____

_____.

forever in my **heart**

These games, TV shows, or sports will always be associated with you in my head:

_____

_____

_____

_____

_____.

Laughing, crying, or just chatting with these people makes me feel as if you're in the room with us, and I know for sure that your spirit is there.

Family members:

_____

_____

_____

_____

_____

Friends:

_____

_____

_____

_____

_____

Coworkers and colleagues:

_____

_____

_____

_____

_____

The best story I recently shared with someone about you was:

_____

_____

_____

_____

_____

_____

_____

_____.

forever in my heart

A funny memory of you I recently laughed about with someone:

_____

_____

_____

_____

_____

_____

_____

_____ .

I described you to someone who has never met you, and this is what I said:

_____

_____

_____

_____

_____

_____

_____

_____ .

I can really see so much of you in this friend or family member:

_____

_____.

They often remind me of you because of these similarities you share:

_____

_____

_____

_____.

There are so many precious keepsakes around the house that I can pick up and hold, or just catch a glimpse of, to bring back memories we've shared, such as _____

_____

_____

_____

_____.

forever in my heart

My favorite thing I bought while on a trip with you out of town is_____

_____

_____

_____.

My favorite thing I bought while on a trip with you out of the country is _____

_____

_____.

Sometimes holding or looking at this object makes me feel close to you, almost like a portal into heaven:_____

_____

_____.

I keep your favorite picture of you here: _____

_____.

It was taken on _____

_____,

and in it you look _____

_____.

I love this picture of you especially because _____

_____

_____

_____.

There are times I can really feel your presence with me, like
when I am doing the following activities that you used to love:

_____

_____

_____

_____.

forever in my heart

I can still feel you here with me when I share the details of my life with you in my thoughts, prayers, and journal entries.

You may be in heaven now, but we can still communicate. My favorite way to tell you what's on my mind or send you a message is _____

_____

_____

_____

_____.

There are some things that happen to me I feel no one will understand or appreciate as much as you, like _____

_____

_____

_____

_____

_____

_____.

Recently this happened, and it made my heart feel heavy:

_____

_____

_____

_____.

When I shared it with you in my thoughts/prayers/journal, I immediately felt _____

_____,

and this is the advice or comforting words I think you might have said to me about the situation if you were still alive: ____

_____

_____

_____

_____.

Even though I can't see your face in front of me, when I share something about my life with you I know you are listening because _____

_____

_____

_____

_____.

forever in my heart

Sometimes after I share something about my life with you I will get a sign from you from heaven, like when this happened:

_____

_____

_____

_____.

You sent me this sign:_____

_____

_____

_____.

When something challenging happens to me or I just get really down, you know about it without my even having to tell you in my thoughts/prayers/journal. Some ways you have shown me you are near me during these times of crisis or sadness are

_____

_____

_____

_____

_____.

The most recent blessing in my life that I shared with you in my thoughts/prayers/journal was _____

_____

_____

_____

_____

_____

You were the first person I wanted to tell when this happened:

_____

_____

_____

_____

_____

_____

forever in my heart

I've had some victories and milestones since you passed, some big and some small. I know you were celebrating along with me from heaven during this special moment:

_____

_____

_____

_____

_____.

At this celebration/party/event/wedding/graduation for

_____,

I invited _____

_____

_____,

and I felt like you were right there raising a glass with us. If you could have given a toast, you probably would have said something like this: _____

_____

_____

_____

_____.

Once I was having difficulty making a decision about

_____

_____

_____,

and I felt like you sent me this sign regarding what to do:

_____

_____

_____.

Once when I shared my problems/fears with you when you
were alive, you gave me this advice, which I still find valuable:

_____

_____

_____

_____

_____

_____.

forever in my **heart**

Just making a conscious effort to contact you through my thoughts/prayers/journal and letting you know what is upsetting me helps because _____

_____

_____

_____

_____.

If you were standing in front of me right now, I'd hug you and wouldn't let go until one of us had to pee. Then I'd tell you this:

_____

_____

_____

_____

_____

_____.

Shhh. It's a secret! This is something I want to share with you that I've never told anyone else before: _____

_____

_____

_____

_____

_____.

Sometimes I communicate with you by saying a daily or occasional blessing for you or sending positive thoughts your way. I usually say or think something like _____

_____

_____

_____

_____.

There are often certain times of the day when I stop and think of you, like_____.

forever in my heart

I think of you especially during this time of day because

_____

_____

_____

_____

_____.

There are times when I make contacting you a little ceremony. There are special places I like to do this, like _____

_____

_____.

This seems like the perfect place to contact you because

_____

_____

_____

_____

_____

_____.

I will play certain music, or light candles, or hold an angel figurine, or _____

_____

_____

_____.

When I share what is on my mind and in my heart with you during these times by speaking aloud, thinking, or praying, afterward I feel _____

_____

_____

_____.

forever in my heart

I can still feel you here with me when the universe sends me love notes from you, special delivery, just when I need them most.

Sometimes I have very vivid dreams about you, almost as if we agreed to meet up at night in a magical land where anything is possible. The most recent dream I had about you was

_____
_____
_____
_____
_____.

You star in so many of my dreams since you've been away, but you could have won an Oscar for this one: _____

_____
_____
_____
_____
_____.

I had this really crazy, silly dream about you since you passed

on: _____

_____

_____

_____

_____

_____

_____.

Sometimes you say or do the most comforting things in my

dreams, like _____

_____

_____

_____

_____

_____

_____.

forever in my heart

Often when I dream about you it feels more real than real life, and it brings back many physical sensations of when you were alive. In my dreams you look like _____

_____,

you feel like _____

_____,

you smell like _____

_____,

and you sound like _____

_____.

Once you gave me advice or a warning in a dream that I really needed to hear. You said, _____

_____

_____,

and this inspired or influenced me to _____

_____

_____

_____

_____.

Could you send me a special dream one night? You don't even have to appear in it. Just send me a dream that makes me feel comforted or gives me insight into challenges I'm currently facing. When I wake up the next morning I'll somehow know intuitively that the dream came from you, and I'll grab this journal and record every detail of the dream here: _____

_____

_____

_____

_____

_____

_____

_____.

I remember a time I'd had a rough day and was especially missing you. You reached out to me unexpectedly by sending me this sign from heaven: _____

_____

_____

_____

_____

_____.

I keep seeing these, and I think it's a sign from you (examples: rainbows, butterflies, angel-shaped clouds, a certain kind of animal, a certain model of car): _____

_____

_____

_____.

I keep hearing this, and I think it's a sign from you (examples: birdsong, a specific ring tone on a phone, a distinctive-sounding car horn, children laughing, wind chimes): _____

_____

_____

_____.

Could you send me a special synchronicity, like seeing the same animal or color, or hearing the same name or word, as a sign that you're thinking of me? When you do I'll jot down the occurrences here and we can smile about them together:

_____

_____

_____

_____

_____.

I've heard your voice whisper in my ear, even though you are worlds away. This is what I've heard you say: _____

_____

_____

_____

_____

_____.

forever in my heart

I was surfing the Web one day, and it was as if you were with me, guiding me to this site or article that I really needed to see:

_____

_____

_____

_____.

Once I was missing you and turned on the TV to find this favorite show/movie of yours playing: _____

_____

_____.

Since you've been gone I've walked into a store or restaurant and this favorite song of ours suddenly came on over the speaker, as if you were DJing:

_____

_____

_____.

Sometime in the future when I'm feeling down or missing you, please send me a special song that I'll hear on the radio or in a store and just know is from you. When I receive this musical message from you I'll come back and record the moment here: _____

_____

_____

_____

_____.

I have felt your physical presence or touch even though you are worlds away. It's hard to describe the experience, but I'll try:

_____

_____

_____

_____

_____

_____

_____

_____.

forever in my heart

Someone posted this picture on social media that seemed like a sign from you: _____

_____

_____

_____

_____.

This weird incident happened with my cell phone and I thought it might be you trying to call from heaven:

_____

_____

_____

_____.

Animals, like furry family pets or cotton candy–colored butterflies, have sent me these signs about you:

_____

_____

_____

_____.

Sometimes I feel as if nature—like the wind through my hair or the sun on my skin—is conspiring to give me this message about you: _____

_____

_____

_____

_____.

I know when I am receiving a sign from you, when it is more than just coincidence or my imagination. I know because of the feeling I get. I'll try to describe this feeling (examples: a chill, hair on my arms stands on end, warm sensations, heart skips a beat, a sense of deep knowing, time seems to stop, energetic shift):

_____

_____

_____

_____

_____

_____.

On these occasions, I was in a store or walking down the street and I thought I saw you: _____

_____

_____

_____

_____

_____.

The most powerful, dramatic sign I've gotten from you since you passed, the one that still gives me chills and brings tears to my eyes, is _____

_____

_____

_____

_____

_____.

I know you are watching and close by whenever I (examples: dance, sing, paint, give a performance, lead a workshop, give a big presentation, bathe the kids, play with the dog, climb a mountain, meditate, spend time in nature) _____

_____

_____

_____

_____.

On this occasion, I got a sign from you or felt you were near me when I was down, and it really cheered me up: _____

_____

_____

_____

_____

_____

_____.

forever in my **heart**

The next time I am celebrating something big, please send me a sign from heaven that you are celebrating too. It will make the celebration that much sweeter when I record your sign here:

_____

_____

_____

_____

_____

_____.

Scrapbook

forever in my **heart**

Scrapbook

CHAPTER 2

You Are Forever in My Heart…
but You Are also in Heaven, and I Am
Trusting That's Where You're Meant to Be

forever in my heart

I understand that you are enjoying yourself
and doing important work in heaven.

I know that Spirit, the angels, and many others watch out
for me from heaven, and I know you are keeping an especially
close eye on me. Here are some of the things I have asked you
for help with since you've been gone: _____

_____

_____

_____

_____

_____.

Here are some of the signs I've gotten/reasons I know that you
were helping me from heaven: _____

_____

_____

_____

_____

_____.

There is something I really need your help with. Can you speak to Spirit and the angels about _____

_____

_____

_____

_____

and ask if they could send me this (or whatever would most help me and be for my highest good): _____

_____

_____.

Can you send me intuitive guidance about this situation? What do I need to know about this situation that I can't see myself?

_____

_____

_____

_____

_____.

(Get quiet and wait for thoughts, feelings, images, words, or gut instincts that might be messages from your loved one.)

And what would help me with this situation that I haven't already thought of or tried myself? _____

_____

_____

_____

_____

_____.

Since we've been apart, it's almost as if you send me little presents as a surprise. There are times when I feel like people or opportunities were brought into my life with your help from heaven, almost as if they arrived wrapped up in a bow with my name on them, like _____

_____

_____

_____

_____

_____.

Even though your time on earth wasn't long enough for me, I can release your soul to heaven knowing you accomplished so much while you were here. Some of your passion projects I am most proud of: _____

_____

_____

_____

_____

_____.

Some of the people you helped and touched deeply while you were alive: _____

_____

_____

_____

_____

_____.

forever in my heart

Work/school projects I am proud of you for accomplishing:

_____

_____

_____

_____

_____.

Before you passed on, it seemed like you might have sensed it was your time to go, or became at peace with your passing. I believe this because _____

_____

_____

_____

_____

_____.

When I am angry that you are far from me, I remember these words that you once told me: _____

_____

_____

_____

_____

_____.

I'm so lucky to have you in my life. Even though we're apart, it's like walking home from the state fair with my arms wrapped around the biggest prize. I'm lucky to have known you when you were alive because _____

_____

_____

_____

_____,

and I'm lucky to have you watching out for me from heaven because _____

_____

_____

_____

_____.

forever in my heart

Some of my favorite character traits of yours that I know are still part of your soul are: _____

_____

_____

_____

_____

_____.

I know you will have a big party arranged for me when I arrive in heaven, and I would like these loved ones who've passed on to be there: _____

_____

_____

_____

_____.

Some of my favorite musicians have passed on, so could you ask the following people to jam at my party when I arrive in heaven: _____

_____

_____

And I'd love for _____

_____

to cook this to eat at my party: _____

_____

_____

When I get to heaven I know you will already be there to show me the ropes and make me feel at home. Maybe you can intuitively give me answers about heaven now. What is it like?

_____

_____

_____

_____

_____

(Get quiet and wait for thoughts, feelings, images, words, or gut instincts that might be messages from your loved one.)

forever in my heart

Give me a hint as to some of your favorite things about heaven:

_____

_____

_____

_____

_____

_____

(Get quiet and wait for thoughts, feelings, images, words, or gut instincts that might be messages from your loved one.)

What will I do when I get to heaven?

_____

_____

_____

_____

_____.

(Get quiet and wait for thoughts, feelings, images, words, or gut instincts that might be messages from your loved one.)

Even though part of me is sad you passed on, another part of
me is glad you are in heaven because (examples: you are out
of pain, you get to see loved ones who passed on that you were
missing) _____

_____

_____

_____

_____

_____.

I think of heaven, or picture heaven, as_____

_____

_____

_____

_____.

I bet you are doing all your favorite things in heaven, like

_____

_____

_____

_____

forever in my heart

While you're in heaven, I am trusting
that right now I'm meant to be here.

I believe the following experiences were part of a grand plan for
my life:

_____

_____

_____

_____

_____

_____

_____

_____

_____

_____.

I think these experiences have helped me grow and enabled me to help others. I'll try to explain: _____

_____

_____

_____

_____

_____

_____

_____

_____

_____ .

I believe the following experiences were part of a grand plan for your life: _____

_____

_____

_____

_____

_____

_____

_____

_____

_____ .

forever in my heart

These are some of the reasons I think you had these experiences, and some of the things I think you learned (examples: compassion, discipline, how to ask for and accept help, self-reliance, furthering your career, finding your calling):

_____

_____

_____

_____

_____

_____

_____.

I believe you were part of the grand plan for my life because

_____

_____

_____

_____

_____

_____

_____

_____.

I believe you being away from me may be part of the plan for us because _____

_____

_____

_____

_____

_____

_____ .

It was a painful lesson, but one of the most valuable things I learned from your passing was _____

_____

_____

_____

_____

_____

_____

_____ .

forever in my heart

Your passing inspired me to make some positive changes in my life, like (examples: take better care of my physical or emotional health, be more adventurous, spend more time with loved ones, go after my dreams, live in the moment)

_____

_____

_____

_____

_____

_____

_____.

Your passing made me see how precious my time on earth is, and these are some ways I want to spend that precious time:

_____

_____

_____

_____

_____

_____

_____

_____.

Some of the biggest items on my bucket list:

_____

_____

_____

_____

_____

_____.

I miss you so much that I wish I could shrink you down, tuck
you in my pocket, and keep you with me all the time. Yet the
following are ways I have grown or changed for the better
because of your absence: _____

_____

_____

_____

_____

_____

_____

_____.

forever in my heart

If I were with you in heaven and not here, I would have missed the chance to _____

_____

_____,

_____

_____

_____,

and _____

_____

_____.

People in my life who need/rely on me: _____

_____

_____

_____

_____

_____

_____.

Places, things, and activities in my life that make my soul sing and my heart swell: _____

_____

_____

_____

_____

_____.

forever in my heart

While you're in heaven, I am
living a full, nourishing life.

Hobbies I'm enjoying lately include: _____

_____

_____

_____

_____

_____.

While you're away, friends, family, and coworkers such as ____

_____,

and _____

have been keeping me company and keeping my chin up.

Being apart from you has made me appreciate the people in my life more, people like _____

_____

_____

_____.

Since you've been gone, spending time with _____

_____

doing _____

_____

helps me unwind and feel easy like Sunday morning.

These days _____

_____

is like laughing gas to me.

Sometimes it feels as though my heart is holding its breath in protest until we're together again, reunited in heaven. When this happens, _____

_____

entices me to open up to life again and savor the moment.

Something new that has come into my life that is meaningful/ joyful is: _____

_____

_____

_____.

My typical Saturday/Sunday since you've been gone looks like this:

_____

_____

_____

_____

_____

_____.

My typical weeknight since we've been apart looks like this:

_____

_____

_____

_____

_____

_____.

Projects at work I've been absorbed in lately: _____

_____

_____

_____

_____

_____.

forever in my **heart**

Projects around the house I'm tackling since you've been away:

_____

_____

_____

_____

_____

_____.

There's a book I fell in love with since we've been apart. It's called

_____

_____.

I love it because _____

_____

_____

_____

_____

_____.

Some films I've watched that touched me or made me laugh since we've been apart: _____

_____

_____

_____

_____

_____.

A favorite line or two of mine from these movies: _____

_____

_____

_____.

A book I read or TV show I saw since you died that reminded me of you: _____

_____

_____.

forever in my heart

There's a character from this book or show that I thought you would especially appreciate: _____

_____

_____.

I find myself listening to the following musical artists a lot lately:

_____

_____

_____

_____.

There's a song I've been playing often these days, around the house or in the car, because it reminds me of you: _____

_____

_____

_____

_____

_____.

Since you've been gone I've spent time outdoors doing

_____

_____

_____

_____

_____.

Since we've been apart I've been processing my emotions by
(examples: journaling, listening to music, creating art, seeing
a counselor, confiding in loved ones, crying, laughing, singing,
dancing) _____

_____

_____

_____

_____

_____

_____

_____.

forever in my heart

Recently I've been taking care of my health by (examples: eating healthy, eating organic, avoiding sugar, limiting my caffeine intake, exercising, meditating, drinking filtered water, going to regular doctor appointments, taking supplements, limiting my stress, nurturing myself, taking breaks from work, playing, getting extra rest) _____

_____

_____

_____

_____

_____

_____.

Some of the biggest life lessons I've learned since you've been gone are _____

_____

_____

_____

_____

_____.

This life lesson in particular was a tough one, and so painful I felt like I was walking around with a Band-Aid on my soul for a while:

_____

_____

_____

_____

_____

_____

_____.

I've experienced a few transformations while we've been apart. In these ways I'm different now _____

_____

_____

_____

_____

_____

_____

_____.

forever in my heart

There are things that I love about myself that I hope will never change, like _____

_____

_____

_____

_____

_____

_____.

Some of the traits that I love most about myself lately:

_____

_____

_____

_____

_____

_____

_____

_____.

Things that I would like to work on or areas for improvement about myself: _____

_____

_____

_____

_____

_____

_____

_____.

I discovered this new side to myself or passion or talent since you've been gone, and it came as a pleasant surprise: _____

_____

_____

_____

_____.

forever in my heart

Some things I want to change about my life are _____

_____

_____

_____

_____

_____

_____.

Something big I know you'd tell me you were proud of me for
accomplishing if you were here: _____ .___

_____

_____

_____

_____

_____.

Something small I know you would tell me you were proud of me for if you were here: _____

_____

_____

_____

_____

_____.

Something I've been regretting lately: _____

_____

_____

_____

_____.

What I love most about my life right now is _____

_____

_____

_____

_____.

Something that makes me excited to get out of bed in the morning:

_____

_____

_____

_____

_____.

Scrapbook

forever in my heart

Scrapbook

CHAPTER 3

You Are Forever in My Heart...
While I'm Thinking of All the
Things I Said to You, and Some
of the Things I Didn't Say

forever in my heart

I love remembering all the love I've expressed to you

One of my favorite ways to tell you I loved you when you were alive was _____

_____

_____

_____.

One of my favorite ways to show you I loved you when you were alive was _____

_____

_____

_____

_____.

When you were alive we were so close that I told you things I didn't share with anyone else, like _____

_____

_____

_____

_____

_____

_____.

One of the reasons I felt so comfortable confiding in you was

_____

_____

_____

_____

_____

_____

_____.

forever in my heart

I remember I used to compliment you all the time about these aspects of your physical appearance: _____

_____

_____

_____

_____

_____.

Something about your personality I used to compliment you on:

_____

_____

_____

_____

_____

_____.

Something about your mind/intellect I often told you I
admired:

_____

_____

_____

_____

_____

_____.

I always remarked upon how talented you were at this, but I
wonder if you ever knew just how good you were:

_____

_____

_____

_____

_____

_____.

forever in my heart

On this occasion, I told you something I thought was unique about you when I felt like you really needed to hear it: _____

_____

_____

_____.

Whenever I gave you a pep talk, I would usually say something like _____

_____

_____

_____

_____

_____

_____.

My pet name(s) for you: _____

_____.

I love remembering all the love
you've expressed to me.

You showed me you loved me in a way I will never forget when:

_____

_____

_____

_____

_____.

My favorite way you used to tell me you loved me:

_____

_____

_____

_____

_____.

forever in my heart

My favorite way you used to show me you loved me:

_____

_____

_____

_____

_____

_____.

A compliment you once gave me that I will always treasure:

_____

_____.

Something you confided to me once that I know you didn't
share with anyone else:

_____

_____

_____

_____

_____

_____.

Something about me that you appreciated/recognized more than anyone else did:

_____

_____

_____

_____

_____.

Something extremely thoughtful you once told me:

_____

_____

_____

_____.

Something very surprising you once told me:

_____

_____

_____

_____

_____

_____.

forever in my **heart**

Something kind you once told me:

_____

_____

_____

_____

_____

_____.

Our favorite times/places to have a heart-to-heart chat:

_____

_____

_____

_____.

I always loved our conversations because

_____

_____

_____

_____

_____

_____.

There are things I wish I would've said to you when you were alive. I would like to say them, and I am ready to say them, now.

There's something I often wish I would have told you before you passed away, but knowing I can still send you messages in heaven, I'll tell you here: _____

_____

_____

_____

_____

_____

_____.

There's something I planned on telling you before you died but I never found the right moment: _____

_____

_____

_____

_____

_____

_____

_____

Something I always wanted to tell you but I felt too ashamed/embarrassed: _____

_____

_____

_____

_____

_____

_____

Knowing you are following along in this journal as I write, the thing I am most inspired to tell you at this moment is:

_____

_____

_____

_____

_____

_____

_____.

Something I kept secret or hidden from you that I wish I would've shared with you when you were alive, or that I am ready to share now: _____

_____

_____

_____

_____

_____

_____

_____.

Something that happened between us I never apologized for:

_____

_____

_____

_____

_____

_____.

Something that happened between us I regret:

_____

_____

_____

_____

_____

_____.

Something I was proud of you for and I never got the chance
to tell you: _____

_____

_____

_____

_____

_____.

There was something I always wanted to say to you, about the
way I feel about you, but I never could quite find the right
words. I'll try to find them now: _____

_____

_____

_____

_____

_____

_____.

forever in my heart

You probably don't know that I sacrificed this for you:

_____

_____

_____

_____

_____

_____.

You hurt me deeply once, but I never expressed it to you. I think it would be healing, for both of us, for me to get my feelings out in the open now: _____

_____

_____

_____

_____

_____

_____

_____.

There's something that happened between us that we never healed while we were both alive, and I'm hoping we can work on healing it now that you are in heaven: _____

_____

_____

_____

_____

_____

_____.

There's something I never asked your forgiveness for when you were alive, but I'd like to ask your forgiveness now for _____

_____

_____

_____

_____

_____

_____.

There is something I wasn't able to forgive you for when you were alive, but since you've passed on I have been able to start forgiving you for _____

_____

_____

_____

_____

_____

_____.

I still have trouble forgiving you for _____

_____

_____

_____,

and when I get quiet and ask Spirit why you hurt me that way, I have a feeling it was because _____

_____

_____

_____

_____.

I tried to tell you what you mean to me when you were alive,
but in case you were unsure, let me tell you again now:

_____

_____

_____

_____

_____

_____

_____

_____.

Something I was scared to tell you when you were alive
because I was nervous about your reaction: _____

_____

_____

_____

_____

_____

_____

_____.

forever in my **heart**

I had some very challenging emotions right before you passed
that I never shared with you. One of my darkest moments was:

_____

_____

_____

_____

_____

_____ .

Something absolutely lovely about you, that I only realized
how much I adored after you passed away and I started missing
you: _____

_____

_____

_____

_____

_____

_____

_____ .

I experienced some unexpected, surprising emotions right before you died, emotions I didn't understand at the time but began to understand much later:

_____

_____

_____

_____

_____

_____

_____

_____.

Something about you that always made me anxious, but I never told you: _____

_____

_____

_____

_____

_____

_____.

forever in my **heart**

Something I kept from you because I felt I was protecting you by not speaking out: _____

_____

_____

_____

_____

_____

_____.

This is something I did for you that I never knew I was capable of, and only my love for you gave me the strength and courage to pull it off: _____

_____

_____

_____

_____.

Scrapbook

forever in my heart

Scrapbook

CHAPTER 4

You Are Forever in My Heart...
and You're Still on My Mind All the Time

forever in my heart

Beautiful memories of you are like my theme song, always playing in the background, setting the tone for my days.

ℛ

My most treasured memory of you, the memory that comes to mind often, a memory that delights me like a sparkling, one-of-a-kind jewel, is _____

_____

_____

_____

_____

_____

_____

_____.

The other day this memory of us suddenly came into my mind and made me laugh out loud: _____

_____

_____

_____

_____

_____.

I was surrounded by people at _____

_____,

when out of the blue my brain conjured up this memory of you: _____

_____

_____

_____

_____,

and even though I was in public I couldn't help but tear up.

My last clear memory of you when you were alive is this:

_____

_____

_____

_____

_____.

Thinking of this last memory of you now makes me feel

_____

_____

_____

because _____

_____

_____

_____.

My most expensive purchase with you was _____

_____

_____

_____,

although it was worth every penny because _____

_____

_____

_____.

I remember this time when we were so merry it seemed as if the day lasted twice as long as normal so we could fit in that much fun, and my heart expanded twice as big as its usual size so I'd be able to feel that much joy: _____

_____

_____

_____

_____

_____.

forever in my heart

I'll never forget the time we went on one of our biggest adventures together, when _____

_____

_____

_____,

and we both got so excited about _____

_____

_____

_____.

The most valuable thing I learned from that adventure was

_____

_____

_____.

During one of our most challenging times together, this is one
memory that really sticks out: _____

_____

_____

_____

_____

_____.

I think from that whole difficult period, this memory of you
sticks out most because _____

_____

_____

_____

_____

_____

_____.

During one of the saddest times of my life, I retain this strong memory of your love, guidance, and support: _____

_____

_____

_____

_____

_____

_____

_____.

You told me something so wise once, it made me wonder if you were a closet philosopher, or an old soul, or channeling some ancient mystic. I still think of these words of yours often:

_____

_____

_____

_____

_____

_____.

I'll always remember the way you handled this situation, because I so admire the maturity/generosity/compassion you displayed:

_____

_____

_____

_____

_____

_____

_____

_____

Since you passed, there is something I did that I dedicated to your memory (examples: dance or speaking performance, garden, work or school project, statue or other piece of art):

_____

_____

_____

_____

_____

It's a lot to sum up here, but basically this is how I remember feeling right after you died: _____

_____

_____

_____

_____

_____

_____

I honor your life and memory each day by (examples: being kind to others, giving people the benefit of the doubt, contributing to charities, standing up for what I believe in, using my natural gifts and talents, working toward my dreams, taking care of my loved ones, taking care of the environment, being kind to animals) _____

_____

_____

_____

_____

_____

_____

_____

The memory of you doing _____

_____

_____

_____

recently inspired me to do this: _____

_____

_____

_____

_____.

When I need courage, I remember the time you _____

_____

_____

_____

_____

_____.

forever in my **heart**

Sometimes we would spend the whole day together. Getting a whole day together was always a treat, and even if we did something ordinary it felt like a decadent indulgence. One of the best days we ever spent together was _____

_____
_____
_____
_____
_____
_____.

Sometimes being around you felt like watching fireworks because _____

_____
_____
_____
_____
_____
_____.

Some of the strongest memories I have of your memorial
service include _____

_____

_____

_____

_____

_____

_____.

One of the saddest memories I have of the time right after you
passed is _____

_____

_____

_____

_____

_____

_____.

forever in my heart

One of the nicest memories I have of the time right after you

passed is _____

_____

_____

_____

_____

_____

_____

_____.

I experienced the privilege of making memories with you while

you were alive for _____ precious years.

Some memories I've made with you as a spirit in heaven (examples: signs you have sent me, times I felt your love or presence, moments I have reached out to you in my thoughts/ prayers/journal):

_____

_____

_____

_____

_____

_____

_____

_____.

Something about you, or something you did, that I never fully understood until after you passed away:

_____

_____

_____

_____

_____

_____

_____.

I have this painful memory of being very angry about your
death right after you passed: _____

_____

_____

_____

_____

_____

_____.

There is something I would like to do in tribute to you. In
your memory and honor, I promise to try my best to

_____

_____

_____,

and I think this would make you happy because _____

_____

_____

_____

_____.

My mind often drifts back to our time together on earth, and I dwell on my favorite details about you.

My favorite thing about your personality:

_____

_____

_____

_____

_____

_____

My favorite thing about your physical appearance:

_____

_____

_____

_____

_____

_____

forever in my heart

Something people were always drawn to you for:

_____

_____

_____

_____

_____

_____.

Something positive people noticed about you right away:

_____

_____

_____

_____

_____.

I used to love it when you smelled like

_____

_____

_____

_____.

Sometimes you would get the funniest expressions on your face. I'll try to describe a few of the most entertaining ones:

_____

_____

_____

_____

_____.

When I close my eyes I can still picture your face. When I close my eyes now and picture you, you look like

_____

_____

_____

_____

_____.

forever in my **heart**

Your sense of humor was so (examples: zany, slapstick, physical, classic, sarcastic, dry) _____

_____,

that it makes me smile right now just to think about it.

You had a very gentle side, which came out when _____

_____

_____

_____

_____

_____.

I would describe your strength as (examples: like a patient lion, like a fierce warrior, like a wise elder) _____

_____

_____

_____

_____

_____.

You knew so much about _____

_____

_____,

and were the smartest person in the room when it came to

_____

_____.

Compassion (examples: came naturally to you, was something you learned, was something that moved you, was something you showed to people you cared about, was something you showed to strangers and the needy, was something that was very important to you)

_____

_____

_____

_____

_____

_____.

I always respected you for valuing this:

_____

_____

_____

_____

_____

_____.

I always admired you for standing up for this: _____

_____

_____

_____.

My favorite thing to see you wearing was _____

_____

_____.

You cooked the best _____

_____,

and I still get a craving for it.

One of the quirkiest things about you was _____

_____

_____

_____,

and I loved you for it because _____

_____

_____

_____.

Sometimes you would get so serious about _____

_____

_____

_____

_____.

forever in my heart

It was so fun to be around you when you'd act silly, like when you would _____

_____

_____

_____

_____

_____.

Scrapbook

forever *in* *my* **heart**

Scrapbook

CHAPTER 5

You Are Forever in My Heart...
and That Has Made Me More
in Touch with My Heart

forever in my heart

I know the most powerful way to experience life is with the heart, like when I explore my emotions, am moved to tears, follow my intuition, or act on my convictions.

I try to stay positive while you're away, but sometimes I miss you so much my heart aches with a pain that is actually physical. The last time I had a good, cleansing cry about your absence was _____

_____

_____

_____

_____

_____

_____.

For me, the hardest part about your death was

_____

_____

_____

_____

_____.

The hardest part about being separated from you is

_____

_____

_____

_____

_____

_____

_____

I don't have a crystal ball, but sometimes I get these strong
intuitive hunches about you: _____

_____

_____

Recently I had this strong intuitive hunch about my life that I
followed: _____

_____

_____

_____

_____

forever in my **heart**

After you left my heart felt so heavy with grief that it was a burden to carry around. This always made me feel lighter:

_____

_____

_____

_____

_____

_____

_____

_____.

Losing you took a toll on my heart, like a car that's seen many miles. I had to take my heart for a tune-up. I started to heal my heart after you left by _____

_____

_____

_____

_____

_____.

I loved that you were so passionate about this when you were alive:

_____

_____

_____

_____

_____

_____

I'm still very passionate about this: _____

_____

_____

_____

Something new I am passionate about since you passed away:

_____

_____

_____

_____

forever in my **heart**

When I am (examples: singing, dancing, writing, riding a bike, riding a horse, hiking in nature) _____

_____,

my heart comes alive and expands so much it's like I can feel the magic and mystery of the whole universe pulsing through my veins.

This is something going on in the world that I feel in my heart is wrong: _____

_____

_____

_____

_____

_____.

And this is what I am doing to try and help: _____

_____

_____

_____

_____.

There is something I feel in my heart I need to take a stand on, but I haven't yet: _____

_____

_____

_____

_____

_____

_____.

I handled this situation recently that I know in my heart I should have handled differently: _____

_____

_____

_____

_____

_____

_____.

forever in my heart

I remember the following time when I followed my heart and things didn't work out the way I'd hoped: _____

_____

_____

_____

_____

_____

_____.

This is what I learned from that situation: _____

_____

_____

_____

_____

_____

_____.

I remember this time when I followed my heart and things turned out better than my wildest dreams: _____

_____

_____

_____

_____

_____

_____.

This was an occasion when my head and heart cooperated perfectly, and the alchemical result was something magical:

_____

_____

_____

_____

_____

_____.

forever in my heart

The heart has answers that the head
could never comprehend. This is
what my heart says about us...

In my heart I know that time is a great healer, because of this
heartbreak from my past that time helped heal:

_____

_____

_____

_____

_____.

I know this, in my heart, about my destiny: _____

_____

_____

_____

_____

_____.

My heart tells me this about the love and affection we shared when you were alive, and still share now: _____

_____

_____

_____

_____

_____

If I could say anything to you right now, straight from the heart, it would be this: _____

_____

_____

_____

_____

_____

_____

_____

forever in my heart

If I get quiet and put my hand over my heart, I can get intuitive messages from my heart. Right now my heart is telling me this about my life: _____

_____

_____

_____

_____.

Could you send me a message straight from your heart to mine? I'll get quiet, put my hand over my heart, and wait for my intuition to tell me what your heart wants mine to know. I think your heart is saying _____

_____

_____

_____

_____.

There is something that has been upsetting me, and when
I get quiet and get in touch with my heart, it beats out this
comforting message: _____

_____

_____

_____

_____

_____.

My heart has the courage of a warrior, and right now it is
nudging me to be brave about _____

_____

_____

_____

_____

_____

_____.

forever in my heart

I know in my heart this is something I need to change about

my life: _____

_____

_____

_____

_____

_____.

Recently I had a major disappointment. When I get quiet, put

my hand over my heart, and ask for some wisdom about why

this happened, my heart tells me _____

_____

_____,

and when I ask my heart about next steps for me regarding

this situation, it advises me to _____

_____

_____

_____

_____.

Sometimes I feel like part of my heart is forever sitting on the front porch like a faithful pooch, watching the horizon for a sign of your return. My heart will never forget you because

_____

_____

_____

_____

_____

_____

_____.

Our hearts are connected to this day, even through time and space, by an invisible bond that can never be broken, like two paper cups connected by a string. That's why my heart can talk to yours anytime, just like the telephone game that kids play. The most important message I feel my heart got from yours since you passed was this: _____

_____

_____

_____

_____

_____

_____.

After you passed, my heart was scared about (examples: living without you, the future in general, my personal safety, my health, where you had gone): _____

_____

_____

_____

_____

_____.

These things help me get in touch with my heart energy (examples: being outside in nature, holding a heart-shaped stone, meditating, being in a calm and quiet place, acting playful, enjoying myself, relaxing, spending time with a child, spending time with an animal, nurturing myself):

_____

_____

_____

_____

_____

_____.

Scrapbook

forever in my heart

Scrapbook

CHAPTER 6

You Are Forever in My Heart...
but I Know that One Day I
Will See You Again

No matter how far apart we are now, I'm certain that one day we will be together again because the bond between us is magnetic.

I have felt the special bond between us, that pulls us together like two planets in mutual orbit, when _____

_____

_____

_____

_____

_____.

I think we share a special bond because _____

_____

_____

_____

_____

_____.

Our connection is unique because _____

_____

_____

_____

_____

_____

_____

_____.

If I could see the energetic bond between us, it would be made up of (examples: colorful flowers, sturdy rope, a glowing gold cord) _____

_____

_____

_____

_____.

I suspect our bond started even before we were born. I think our souls conspired to come to earth together, and these are some of the things I think we planned to do: _____

_____

_____

_____

_____

_____ .

The dictionary defines the word "bond" as "something shared between people that creates a connection." This is how I would define our bond, or some words I would use to describe it:

_____

_____

_____

_____

_____

_____ .

Some things that happened when you were alive that
strengthened our bond: _____

_____

_____

_____

_____

_____

_____.

Events that occurred after you passed that strengthened our
bond:

_____

_____

_____

_____

_____

_____.

forever in my **heart**

Something happened that weakened our bond, but once we worked through this situation and our feelings, we came back together and our bond was stronger than ever: _____

_____

_____

_____

_____

_____.

I have big plans for us when we are reunited!

The next time I see you and can put my arms around you,
I've got a Hollywood-movie-style montage planned for us. The
theme song will be _____

_____,

and in some of the scenes we will _____

_____,

and _____

_____.

Someday when my time on earth is over and all the work
Spirit wanted me to do in this lifetime is complete, we will
be reunited in heaven. Besides you, the following are some
loved ones who are already in heaven that I am most looking
forward to seeing:

_____

_____

_____

_____

_____

_____.

These are some great thinkers, famous artists, brilliant scientists, important world leaders, passionate activists, and generally interesting folks through the ages who have passed on that I would also love to meet when it's my time to go to heaven: _____

_____
_____
_____
_____
_____.

The first meal I would like for us to have together in heaven would be _____

_____
_____
_____
_____
_____.

People who've had near-death experiences describe heaven as being sublimely beautiful, and perhaps since it's heaven, there can be countless terrains, any type I fancy: mountains, beaches, deserts, forests. I think I would prefer to meet with you in heaven in this kind of nature setting: _____

_____

_____

_____

_____

_____

People who've had these near-death experiences often describe seeing fields of flowers in heaven. If I could run through any sort of field in heaven and have you waiting at the other end, it would be a field filled with this kind of flower: _____

_____

_____

_____

_____

_____.

forever in my heart

Some activities I would love to do together in heaven when we are reunited:

_____

_____

_____

_____

_____

_____.

Can you let the following ascended masters, mystics, and spiritual pioneers who have passed over know that when I get to heaven I would love to meet with them face-to-face?

_____

_____

_____

_____

_____

_____.

The first thing I will whisper in your ear when I see you in heaven is

_____

_____

_____

_____

_____

_____.

forever in my heart

Scrapbook

Scrapbook

forever in my heart

CHAPTER 7

You Are Forever in My Heart...
and So Are the Dreams We've Shared

Every dream we dreamed together
is a precious memory for me.

We had dreams that worked out, and some that didn't. One
of the dreams we had that came true beyond our wildest
imaginations was _____

_____

_____

_____

_____

_____

_____.

This big dream we had didn't work out at all, and you were so
good at comforting me and helping me think of a brand-new
dream to go after: _____

_____

_____

_____

_____

_____.

forever in my heart

A dream we shared didn't turn out as we'd planned, and it became obvious later that this was a blessing in disguise:

_____

_____

_____

_____

_____

_____.

This was a big dream of mine that I never could have accomplished without your help: _____

_____

_____

_____

_____

_____.

This was a dream I initially didn't have the courage to go after, but you inspired me to try: _____

_____

_____

_____

_____

_____.

This was one of your dreams I saw you go after with gusto when you were alive. You worked so hard for this dream and sacrificed so much. The pride and joy I felt when this dream came true for you made me feel like it was my dream too:

_____

_____

_____

_____

_____

_____.

forever in my heart

You had a dream that didn't come true, and even though you were so hurt and disappointed, you handled it with such grace and wisdom. I admired how you dealt with this setback:

_____

_____

_____

_____

_____

_____.

This dream came true because of opportunities, ideas, resources, and people that came our way and made it obvious Spirit was watching this situation very closely:

_____

_____

_____.

Some things/people that helped us accomplish this dream that I'm sure were divinely sent:

_____

_____

_____

_____.

While you've been in heaven and I've been here on earth, I've kept on dreaming.

Right after you passed, it was hard for me to dream big and set new goals. But these were some things that happened that encouraged me to get back in the flow of life, and start dreaming again about ways to change and improve my life and help others:

_____

_____

_____

_____

_____

_____.

Someone (or people) in my life right now who encourages me to dream big for myself:

_____

_____

_____

_____

_____

_____.

My most cherished, sacred dream for my life right now is

_____

_____

_____

_____

_____

_____.

A dream I have that I'm nervous or afraid to share with
anyone yet is _____

_____

_____

_____

_____

_____.

A current dream I have for my life that is making me grow
and stretch so far it feels like I will have to stretch up to the
sky to reach this goal is _____

_____

_____

_____

_____

_____.

Some smaller goals I have for myself right now, like little pieces of glitter that will make my daily life more dazzling, are

_____

_____

_____

_____

_____

_____.

If I could wish upon a star and have any dream come true for you in heaven, I would say, "Star light, star bright, I wish I may, I wish I might, have this wish I wish tonight":

_____

_____

_____

_____

_____.

Some things I could use Spirit's help with right now to accomplish my dreams (examples: financial stability, less drama at home, less drama at work, more free time, more help, more confidence, more opportunities, a mentor):

_____

_____

_____

_____

_____

_____.

I know sometimes a subconscious block can hinder people from going after their dreams. When I ask my intuition to tell me if there are any subconscious reasons I am scared to go after my dreams, or scared of having my dreams come true, this is what I learn: _____

_____

_____

_____

_____

_____

_____

Scrapbook

Scrapbook

forever in my heart

CHAPTER 8

You Are Forever in My Heart...
and We Are Both Surrounded by Angels

I know heaven is full of angels, but there are also humans walking around earth who acted angelically to us in our hour of need.

Those months, weeks, days, or hours before you passed were made more bearable, and more peaceful, by the presence of these friends and loved ones: _____

_____

_____

_____

_____

_____.

The following doctors, nurses, and other healthcare professionals acted as earth angels to us after you got sick/ injured: _____

_____

_____

_____

_____

_____.

forever in my heart

I don't think I could have made it through watching you die without this human angel by my side: _____

_____.

I think this angelic person helped you the most during your soul's transition to heaven: _____

_____.

While you were dying, this person was always there when I needed someone to talk to: _____

_____.

I would like to ask divine angels to help me process my emotions. Some emotions I still have trouble dealing with since your death include (examples: anger, sorrow, denial, frustration, loneliness, guilt, shame, regret, shock, nervousness):

_____

_____

_____.

While you're in heaven, human angels are watching over me.

After you passed, when I felt like I couldn't go on, this person picked me up and carried me, as if on angel's wings:

_____

_____.

After you left, this person brought me out into the light again, like an angel revealing to me the brilliant light of Spirit, and helped me continue living: _____

_____.

This human angel helped me make sense of your passing and helped me process all the intense emotions I had after you died: _____

_____.

If I were to ask Spirit to send me a human angel right now, I'd ask for someone who could help me with _____

_____.

This human angel in my life right now reminds me of you:

_____.

This human angel in my life helps me keep your memory alive:

_____.

This human angel in my life challenges me to be my best:

_____.

This person in my life right now makes me so happy I almost think they must be an angel: _____

_____.

I have been blessed by so many human angels over the course of my life, and I'll try to remember some of them now:

_____

_____

_____

_____

_____

_____

_____

forever in my heart

Scrapbook

Scrapbook

forever in my **heart**

Conclusion

I hope you enjoyed filling out this guided journal. But remember, the journey doesn't stop here! Not only can you go back and leaf through your completed journal to savor memories of your loved one or simply feel closer to them, you can also communicate with your loved one anytime, anyplace, in countless ways. Buy a blank journal and write your loved one a letter whenever you are missing them, let your loved one know through your prayers or thoughts that they're on your mind, serenade your loved one by singing along to a song on the radio, visit one of your loved one's favorite places, dedicate a project to your loved one, take a walk in nature and ask your loved one's spirit to accompany you, celebrate your loved one's birthday, or whisper a request to your loved one for signs of their continued presence in your life.

Death is not the end of your relationship with your loved one, nor is it merely a temporary separation until you are reunited in heaven. Death can be an invitation to begin a completely new relationship with your loved one. Get curious and excited about what that relationship could be like. In some ways this new relationship with your loved one is limited compared to the relationship you had when they were still alive. But in other ways it is limitless! A relationship that, due to its unique nature, has its own unique blessings. Feeling that the deep connection to your loved one still exists, and sensing their strong presence in your life, can bring you to a whole new level of faith and wonder about this magical adventure our souls are on. Things that were hidden or unsaid between you and your loved one during life can be more easily shared since your loved one's passing, and issues that seemed too difficult to resolve with your loved one when they were alive can be resolved now.

As a professional intuitive, I've had many souls in heaven give me messages to share with their loved ones on earth. One of the most powerful lessons I have learned in my Angel Readings with clients is this: Loved ones who pass on very much want to make contact with you and let you know that they are still watching you, and still loving you, from heaven. This is what inspired me to set out one morning for a very old chapel in my neighborhood, kneel down at its altar, and say a special prayer. "Spirit," I asked, "please help me create a bridge between heaven and earth so that souls in heaven can connect with their loved ones here." This journal is that bridge, the answer to my prayer. My wish is that this journal has been an answer to your prayers as well.

Acknowledgments

The author would like to thank her excellent agent, Linda Konner, who had the original idea for this guided journal, as well as her husband, her family, her friends, and especially her angels. The author would also like to thank Bridget Thoreson, Casie Vogel and everyone at Ulysses Press for making this project possible.

About the Author

Tanya Carroll Richardson is a self-improvement/spiritual author and professional intuitive who is passionate about angels, beauty, and nature. She has been writing about angels, and interviewing people about their encounters with angels, for over a decade. She is also the author of *Angel Insights: Inspiring Messages From, and Ways to Connect With, Your Spiritual Guardians* (Llewellyn Worldwide) and *Heaven on Earth: A Guided Journal for Creating Your Own Divine Paradise* (Sterling Ethos). Learn more about Tanya's private Angel Readings, or follow her on social media, by visiting tanyarichardson.com.